Colour of
A Lancashire
Triangle

Colour of
A Lancashire
Triangle

By Dennis Sweeney

TRIANGLE

PUBLISHING

Copyright © D.J. Sweeney 1998.
First published by Triangle Publishing
British Library Cataloguing in Publishing/data
Sweeney D.J.

Colour of A Lancashire Triangle
ISBN 0952933330

Printed in Great Britain by the
Amadeus Press Ltd. Huddersfield.

Text by D.J.Sweeney.

Compiled by
Scene Print & Design Ltd., Leigh.

Designed & Published by
Triangle Publishing,
509 Wigan Road,
Leigh,
Lancs.

01942/677919.

Cover Photo.

Stanier Pacific No.46229 "Duchess of Hamilton" entered traffic in
September 1938, as one of the red streamliners. De-streamlining occured
in December 1947, but still retaining the sloping smokebox until February
1957. The livery sported by 46229, seen here at Wigan North Western in
1958, is that as applied in September of that year, maroon with B.R. style
lining set in from the edges, with the second B.R. emblem on the tender.
The locomotive is almost certainly ex-works and is admired by schoolboy
spotters. **(See also Plate 14, page 15).**   *Photo, B.Nichols.*

By the same Author:

A Lancashire Triangle Part One.
Features the Bolton & Leigh and Kenyon & Leigh Junction Railways and the
first ever survey of the Eccles-Tyldesley-Wigan branch.
ISBN 0952933306. 192pp, 237 b&w prints, plus maps and line drawings,
hardback, colour jacket, price £25.00.

A Lancashire Triangle Part Two.
Covers the Tyldesley-Leigh-Pennington-Bickershaw Junction route and
Roe Green to Bolton Great Moor Street.
No survey of South Lancashire's railways would be complete without some
reference to the once numerous industrial railways of the area.
Bickershaw, Gin Pit, Central Railways and more, are all covered.
ISBN 0952933322, 200pp, 230 b&w prints, line maps, diagrams, full colour
jacket, hardback, price £25.00.

CONTENTS

The Bolton & Leigh Railway   P. 6

Wigan to Manchester Exchange   P.15

Tyldesley - Leigh - Bickershaw   P.27

The Industrial Scene   P.44

8F, 48491 near Hulton Sidings.   *Photo, J.R.Carter.*

"Colour of A Lancashire Triangle;" intended primarily as a supplement to the successful "Lancashire Triangle" Parts One & Two, and depicting colour scenes within the area covered by those volumes.

Save for the truncated Bickershaw branch, all the railways featured within closed long ago. Chequerbent, Patricroft, Jackson's Sidings; names once familiar to generations of railwaymen. Locations which echoed to the crash of buffers and the sight and sound of the steam locomotive.

In many respects I feel priveledged to have witnessed at first hand the steam locomotives in action at these and other forgotten places. To have seen with my own eyes the gleaming ex-works Jubilees, Scots or Britannias on the Windermere or Glasgow expresses; grimy 8F's or Class 5"s struggling with heavy coal trains, (or, in the case of Chequerbent, the not so heavy) and the inevitable Patriot working the 7.05.p.m. Liverpool Road-Carlisle goods.

No photographs can ever replace those memories but for those too young and those not fortunate enough to have observed these events, this small publication will, I am sure, illustrate just how much they have missed. It will also allow the rest to wallow knee deep in nostalgia and reflect upon the folly which saw mile after mile of valuable railway infrastructure thrown on the scrapheap.

It is inevitable that there are some bare areas where, despite my efforts, the elusive colour shot remains just that. Roe Green to Bolton via Little Hulton is one such area, but I am equally sure that when this book appears in print the missing views will surface. Sod's Law ordains it!

Once again I take this opportunity to express my thanks to all those who have provided information and material for inclusion.

D.J.Sweeney,
Leigh, 1998.

THE BOLTON & LEIGH RAILWAY

Plate 1. It is appropriate to begin a colour survey of the "Triangle" at, or as near as possible, to the location which saw Stephenson's *Lancashire Witch* depart Pendlebury Fold for Bolton on the opening day of the Bolton & Leigh Railway, 1st August 1828.

Stanier 8F No.48491 is seen at Booth's Siding in 1963 after working a trip freight from Bag Lane, Atherton, to Booths. Hulton Sidings signal box can be seen to the rear of the locomotive. Over on the right is the concrete works at Pendlebury Fold, this built on a site formerly occupied by one of Wm.Hulton's collieries which in those far off Bolton & Leigh days supplied coal for Bolton markets.

Photo, J.R.Carter.

Plate 2. From the footplate., the Driver of an 8F, with hand on the regulator, keeps a watchfull eye to the rear of his train whilst shunting at Hulton Sidings in January 1968.

Photo, D.Hill.

Plate 3. Arriving at Hulton Sidings in Easter 1968, are a Type 4 Diesel and a Class 8F, seen after double heading up Chequerbent Bank. Hulton Sidings was, by this period, the extent of the railway toward Bolton, Hulton Sidings - Bolton having closed in October 1967. Hulton Sidings-Howe Bridge East Junction was to close on 6th January 1969, thus bringing to an end Stephenson's historic railway. *Photo,D.Hill.*

Plate 4. At the head of an enthusiast's special is 8F No.48178 seen passing Chequerbent Yard. Chequerbent Station had closed in October 1952 but the signal cabin at this location, seen on the left, remained open until May 1965.

The railtour in question was the LCGB's (N.W.Branch) "South Lancashire Limited," of Saturday, 21st September 1963. The tour began at Liverpool Road Goods Station, Manchester, this the original terminus of the Liverpool & Manchester Railway which had opened on 15th September 1830.

Within the itinerary of the tour were a number of South Lancashire's railways under threat of closure, including the remaining section of former Bolton & Leigh Railway, from Atherton to the environs of Crook Street Goods Yard, Bolton, where reversal, and a change of motive power, took place. "Jinty" 0-6-0 No.47378, taking over for the short journey to Little Hulton Junction and back. Later in the day, parts of the former Great Central route to Wigan and St Helens, plus the Bickershaw Junction-Kenyon Junction route would also be traversed.

Photo, D.Hill

Plate 5. Ex W.D. 2-8-0, No.90493 climbs Chequerbent Bank unassisted with a short freight as the fireman catches sight of the photographer.

Photo, D.Hill.

Plate 6. The climb from Bag Lane to Chequerbent was notoriously steep. Officially the gradient was 1 in 30 but mining subsidence increased this to 1 in 18 and in the final years of operation a number of former railwaymen suggest it became worse. In April 1968, 8F No.48339, is seen giving banking assistance to a train of hoppers worked by another 8F. On the right had been Stephenson's original alignment of 1828, later used by Wm. Hulton's colliery locomotives to access their mines at Chequerbent. *Photo, D.Hill.*

Plate 7. Stanier 8F, No.48327 and Standard Class 5 No.73040, arrive at Bag Lane, Atherton, with stone hoppers for Pendlebury Fold in April 1968, as 8F No.48339 shunts the yard. Here, trains would be re-marshalled, and reduced considerably in payload for the ascent of Chequerbent Bank.

Photo, D,Hill.

Plate 8. Standard Class 5 No.73040 at Bag Lane as 8F No.48327 draws forward.

Photo, D.Hill.

Plate 9. A view south toward Bag Lane and Leigh from Chequerbent about 1960. In the middle distance is the former Lancashire & Yorkshire's Pendleton-Atherton Central-Crow Nest Junction, Hindley, route opened in 1888, which passed beneath the Chequerbent line in a cutting and is largely hidden from view. Distinguishing landmarks of yesteryear are, on the left, Laburnum Mill, Atherton., on the right, Lancashire United's Transport Depot at Howe Bridge and in the distance the numerous factory or mill chimneys of Leigh.

Photo, D.Hill.

Plate 10. Between Chequerbent and Bag Lane the railway crossed the Lancashire & Yorkshire's four track Pendleton-Crow Nest Junction route. During a snow flurry in December 1967, an unidentified 8F descends Chequerbent Bank toward Bag Lane with a freight from Hulton Sidings. The view is taken from North Road, Atherton, looking east toward Hag Fold.

Photo, D.Hill.

Plate 11. The area around Pennington Junctions had been notorious for flooding over a period of many years. This view from St Helens Road, looking east across the former Kenyon & Leigh Junction Railway at Pennington, c1965, shows the railway totally submerged beneath the flooded landscape. Note the Kenyon home signal in the "off" position; for the boat train perhaps....!   *Photo, D.Norman.*

Plate 12. Appropriately, the final acts of B.R. steam operations were played out in the North West of England and an endless procession of steam specials traversed the ancient metals of Chat Moss, including the famous, or infamous, depending on your point of view, 15 guinea special on 11th August 1968. This view at Kenyon Junction on 4th August 1968, depicts Stanier Class 5, No.45305 seen passing Kenyon No.1 box en-route to Liverpool Lime Street. Although the junction for Leigh and Tyldesley remained in use, by this date Kenyon sidings had been lifted.   *Photo, P.Hampson*

Plate 13. By the time this view at Kenyon Junction was taken in mid 1964, Kenyon Yard no longer echoed to the hustle and bustle of freight shunting movements, except for the odd coal train stabled overnight or the sludge train from the nearby water softening plant. Goods facilities were withdrawn the previous year and the passenger station closed on 2nd January 1961. 9F No.92019, waits for the right away at Kenyon with a coal train from Jackson's Sidings, Tyldesley, bound for Margam, South Wales. *Photo, J.R.Carter.*

NEW PUBLICATIONS FROM THE MOSELEY RAILWAY TRUST

A GUIDE TO SIMPLEX NARROW GAUGE LOCOMOTIVES

By David Hall and John Rowlands

This 112-page book includes a history of the Motor Rail & Tramcar Company from its beginnings in 1911 to the end of locomotive production at Bedford and the sale of the locomotive business to Alan Keef Ltd. The historical material includes information resulting from interviews with former employees as well as surviving archive material. All true narrow gauge types are covered and the works-number series of each type is listed. It is fully illustrated with 86 black & white photographs, 23 scale drawings (which will be suitable for modelling purposes), and 11 other illustrations. The book is professionally printed and bound using 130 gsm gloss art paper with a page size of 176mm x 235mm.

When published it will be priced in soft-back at £10.95, with a limited edition of 150 hardback copies priced at £16.95.

SPECIAL OFFER. Orders placed and paid for before the **10th of October 2001.**
Soft-back Edition **£9.95** including UK post and packing. Overseas £1 P&P
Hard-back Edition **£16.95** including UK post and packing. Overseas £1 P&P
Publication date is approximately mid October, and advance orders will be despatched within 2 weeks of publication. Cheques <u>must</u> reach us before the 10th October to guarantee this offer.

PEAT MOSS RAILWAYS OF BRITAIN

by David Hall and Ken Scanes with plans and drawings by Jeremy Tilston

This book details the known narrow gauge railways that have been used to harvest peat in England, Scotland and Wales. It covers peat and its uses, harvesting methods, and the railways and rolling stock. A gazetteer features known details of each of the sites and lists the locomotives known to have worked at each location. It is published in A5 format and contains 74 quality laser printed pages, tape bound with 54 black & white photographs, 3 drawings, and 12 track plans. Price £4.95 + Post & packing: UK 50p, EU £1.00, Rest of the world £2.00

Payment should be made in Sterling drawn on a UK bank or a Eurocheque, Cheques should be made payable to "MOSELEY RAILWAY TRUST" and sent with your order to ;-

MRT (Publications) 11 Ashwood Road Disley Cheshire, SK12 2EL United Kingdom	A Guide to Simplex Locomotives (please state quantity) Peat Moss Railways of Britain (please state quantity) Total payment £............	Hard-back ☐ Soft-back ☐

Limited Credit Card Payment facilities exist for **OVERSEAS CUSTOMERS ONLY**
Mastercard / Visa (delete as appropriate)
Credit Card Number..Expiry Date.................
Signature............................

Name.. Address..................................

....

Post code................. Country.....................................

Colour of a Lancashire Triangle   Index
_____

Page No.   Plate No.   Plate No. of colliery locos

1D

Map	64		
Wigan North Western	Covers 14 16		
Springs Branch & area	16 18		
Wigan — Tyldesley	16—22		
Bickershaw Jc.	19 20		
" Colliery + loco	54—61	64—9	84
Bolton + Leigh Rly	S 1—10	62 63	
Pennington	11 53		
Kenyon Junction	12 13		
Leigh	39—52		
Speakman's Sidings, Leigh	36—8		
Jackson's " Tyldesley	32—5		
Parsonage Colliery	70		
Astley Green "	71—5		
Mosley Common "	76—7		
NCB Walkden	78—81		
" Little Hulton	82		
Sanderson's Sidings Worsley	23 83		
Patricroft shed	24—9		
Eccles	30		
Manchester Exchange	31		

Plate 14. The cabside lining shows up well in this forward facing view as 46229 prepares to depart Wigan North Western with an Up express.

Photo, B. Nichols.

Plate 15. Wet days didn't put off the train spotters as this view in the long gone bay platforms at Wigan illustrates. One of the B.R., Derby Works units also attracts the interest of footplate staff prior to departing for Liverpool Lime Street about 1958. *Photo, B.Nichols.*

Plate 16. The route to Manchester Exchange from Wigan North Western diverged at Springs Branch, Manchester Lines Junction, closing to through traffic on 5th. May 1969. In October 1985, Type 4, No 97 407 *Aureol*, formerly D212, is seen on the stub end of the former Up Goods line prior to accessing Springs Branch with P.W. vehicles. The single track of railway continued to Bickershaw Colliery for coal traffic and at the time of writing is still in situ.

Photo, Author.

17

Plate 17. On 5th August 1974, Type 2, No.25 247 is seen west of Bickershaw Junction, with a coal train from Howe Bridge West Sidings, passing over the former Great Central's Glazebrook-Wigan Central route which had closed a few years earlier. *Photo, Ian Isherwood.*

Plate 18. Here's one for the prototype modellers to attempt! A rather delapidated looking Type 4, No.D342 is seen going on shed at Springs Branch on 16th February 1970. This is another Vulcan Foundry built locomotive having entering service in May 1961, renumbered to 40 142 in May 1974, but withdrawn in April 1980 and cut up at Crewe three years later. *Photo, Ian Isherwood.*

Plate 19. Bickershaw Junction on 3rd September 1970 as Type 4, No.D206 arrives with a train of empties for Abram North Exchange Sidings. The metal footbridge gave pedestrian passage over this once busy location but was demolished many years ago. D206 was one of the first batch of this type to enter service, in July 1958, later becoming 40 006 and withdrawn in 1983. *Photo, Ian Isherwood.*

Plate 20. The footbridge gave a good view of the surrounding area as in this view eastward, toward Howe Bridge, with Scowcroft's Tip in the background. The line to Abram and Bickershaw Colliery goes off to the right. After working empties to Abram on 21st September 1971, Type 2, No.7635 is about to propell the brake van to Howe Bridge West Sidings, then the extent of the former through route via Tyldesley to Eccles Junction. *Photo, Ian Isherwood.*

Plate 21. Shortly after the end of steam working on B.R., Type 2, No.5257 is seen east of Howe Bridge Station with an engineer's train for Patricroft. Opencast mining operations in the 1980's have removed all trace of the railway at this location. *Photo, Ian Isherwood.*

Plate 22. A Stanier 8F with a Type 4 diesel locomotive in tow, seen passing over Astley Steet, Tyldesley, just east of Tyldesley Station. Note the timber shoreing under the bridge which had been in place longer than anyone could remember.

Photo, D.Hill.

Plate 23. A pair of 8F's, Nos. 48663 & 48720 have arrived at Sanderson's Sidings, Worsley, with a coal train from Speakman's Sidings, Leigh, and are seen propelling the train into the sidings for onward transportation to Sandhole Washery by N.C.B. locomotives. Note the brake van standing on the Up line near Sanderson's cabin. When shunting is completed, engines and van will work to Patricroft.

Photo, J.R.Carter.

Plate 24. Footplate skills and photography were only two of railwayman Jim Carter's attributes as this elevated view illustrates, for surely it required the agility of a mountain goat and the heart of a lion to attain the necessary altitude to take this shot from the top of Patricroft's coaling plant. Viewed toward Eccles, a 9F is seen on the ash pit as a 2-6-2T gently meanders by. Two 8F's are also in view, as a Britannia departs from North Sidings. A diesel shunter rests near the shunters cabin and at top right can be seen "Four Bridges."

Plate 25. A nicely posed view of Royal Scot No.46169 *The Boy Scout* at Patricroft about 1962. The engine will work one of the afternoon express trains from Manchester Exchange.

Photo, J.R.Carter.

Plate 26. Stanier Class 5, No.44767 is seen shunting a dead Standard Class 5 for boiler washout at Patricroft. 44767 is now preserved. *Photo, J.R.Carter.*

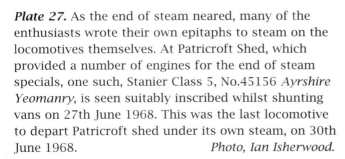

Plate 27. As the end of steam neared, many of the enthusiasts wrote their own epitaphs to steam on the locomotives themselves. At Patricroft Shed, which provided a number of engines for the end of steam specials, one such, Stanier Class 5, No.45156 *Ayrshire Yeomanry*, is seen suitably inscribed whilst shunting vans on 27th June 1968. This was the last locomotive to depart Patricroft shed under its own steam, on 30th June 1968. *Photo, Ian Isherwood.*

Plate 28. Britannia Pacific No.70010 arrived at Patricroft after working a running in turn from Crewe. The engine has run tender first from Manchester, as indicated by the tail lamp, possibly having worked a Scottish fish train south. Note that the locomotive has been out-shopped in plain green, minus its *Owen Glendower* nameplates. Photo, *J.R.Carter.*

Plate 29. 8F No.48720 catches the light whilst on shed at Patricroft in the mid 1960's. This was a regular engine on the heavy coal trains from Jackson's or Speakman's Sidings in the last years of steam. It can still be seen working coal trains through Tyldesley, albeit in 4mm scale, on the Author's model railway. Photo, *J.R.Carter.*

Plate 30. Ex-Crosti 9F, No.92022, propells a freight down gradient at Stott Lane, Eccles, toward Manchester Ship Canal Sidings about 1965. One of a batch of ten built with Italian designed Franco-Crosti boilers in 1955, 92022 is seen after conversion to standard as the experiment to achieve greater steam efficiency was deemed a failure by B.R.

Photo, J.R.Carter.

Plate 31. Manchester Exchange about 1962 as Ex-LNWR "Super D" No.49323 plods toward Ordsall Lane on the through road with a freight from Huddersfield. The station was demolished at the end of the steam era and is now a car park but in its heyday, together with Manchester Victoria's half, was home to the world's longest platform.

Photo, J.R.Carter.

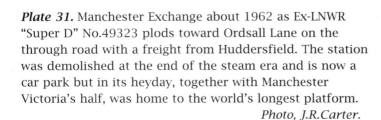

TYLDESLEY-LEIGH-BICKERSHAW

Plate 32. 9F, No.90219 is seen in Jackson's Sidings, Tyldesley, ready to depart with a coal train for Margam, South Wales in mid 1964. Driver Cliff Davies keeps an eye on the rear of his train whilst Fireman Jim Carter attends to the camera work. Jackson's Sidings signal cabin is seen at top left. **(See also Plate 13.)**

Plate 33. The gradient from Jackson's Sidings to Tyldesley was officially 1 in 100. However, again mining subsidence increased this, particularly in the last years of the railway. About 1965, a heavy coal train from Jacksons approaches Tyldesley and is shot from the banking engine, a Stanier 8F. Note the distant signal for Tyldesley at caution, probably to allow a Leigh-Manchester Exchange passenger train to clear the station as by this period the Wigan-Manchester Exchange passenger service had been withdrawn. *Photo, J.R.Carter.*

Plate 34. Having propelled her train out onto the main line from Jackson's Sidings, 8F No.48322 stands wrong road awaiting clearance to depart for Patricroft. Sister engine No.48720 will provide the banking assistance up the 1/100 incline to Tyldesley when a Liverpool Lime Street-Manchester Exchange DMU has cleared section.

Photo, J.R.Carter.

28

Plate 35. A B.R. Standard Class 5, banked by an 8F, are seen passing Jackson's Sidings with an early morning coal train from Speakman's Sidings, Leigh, about 1965. The signals show a clear road through Tyldesley and both engines are hard at work. *Photo, J.R.Carter.*

Plate 36. Speakman's Sidings, Leigh, c1965, as 8F, No.48720, and brake van, stand, waiting for their train to be made up by the colliery locomotive. The second B.R. emblem, nicknamed "Ferret & Dartboard" by engine spotters, is clearly seen on the tender of this exceptionally clean 8F. Lilford Park woods are on the left.   *Photo, J.R.Carter.*

Plate 37. A Sundays, Newcastle-Liverpool Lime Street diversion via Eccles Junction, Tyldesley, Leigh and Kenyon Junction, is worked by Peak Class No.D175, and is seen passing the now dissused Speakman's Sidings on 19th January 1969. *Photo, Ian Isherwood.*

Plate 38. A three car, Birmingham Carriage & Wagon Co. DMU, Nos.M50521.M59177 & M50469, pass Speakman's Sidings on 3rd September 1968, bound for Manchester Exchange. By this late period, Speakman's signal box had been abolished leaving Leigh, Tyldesley and Monton Green as the only operable cabins on the through Kenyon-Leigh-Tyldesley-Eccles Junction route.

Photo, Ian Isherwood.

Plate 39. West of Speakman's Sidings, a green Peak, No.D182, is also seen on a Newcastle-Lime Street diversion on 2nd February 1969, and is photographed from the Lilford Park footbridge known locally as "Iron Bridge." These Type 4's were built by B.R. at Derby between October 1961 and January 1963, and were later to become Class 46 under the tops re-numbering scheme. This particular example, No.46 045 was withdrawn from service in November 1984, to enter departmental stock as No.97 404.
Photo, Ian Isherwood.

Plate 40. A Liverpool Lime Street-Newcastle diversion, hauled by Type 4 No.D1614, approaches Iron Bridge on 13th October 1968. This locomotive received its first tops number, No.47 034, in March 1974, was re-numbered to 47 561 in October 1980, to departmental use as No.97 561 in September 1988, and re numbered yet again to 47 973 in July 1989. Between May 1989 and March 1990, it carried the name *Midland Counties Railway 150, 1839-1989.* In September 1990, was re-named *Derby Evening Telegraph.* *Photo, A.Yates.*

Plate 41. At same spot, a snow scene of February 1967, as a three car DMU approaches with the service for Manchester Exchange. *Photo, A.Yates.*

Plate 42. The same location, near Iron bridge in October 1968, is a Metro Cammell unit with the all round stripe approaches en-route to Manchester.

Photo, A.Yates.

Plate 43. On 26th. May 1968, a two car DMU is seen on the approach to Leigh and is about to cross Holden Road bridge.

Photo, A.Yates.

Plate 44. Between Iron Bridge and Holden Road overbridge there was a crossing known to locals as "White Gates" . A Trans-Pennine unit in the B.R. corporate blue livery approaches the crossing in 1968 with a Sunday, Ex- Lime Street diversion. The signals in the background mark the location of the next shot.

Photo, A.Yates.

Plate 45. One of the Park Royal units Nos.M56151 & M50403 are seen running alongside Rosebury Avenue, Leigh, with a Manchester Exchange service on 5th September 1968. Holden Road Bridge and Leigh signal box are seen in the background.

Photo, Ian Isherwood.

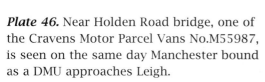

Plate 46. Near Holden Road bridge, one of the Cravens Motor Parcel Vans No.M55987, is seen on the same day Manchester bound as a DMU approaches Leigh.

Photo, Ian Isherwood.

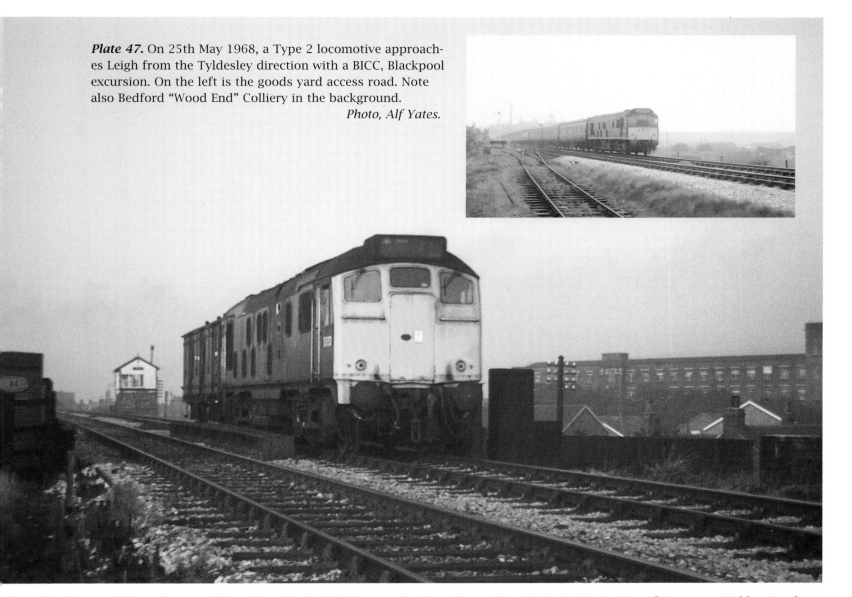

Plate 47. On 25th May 1968, a Type 2 locomotive approaches Leigh from the Tyldesley direction with a BICC, Blackpool excursion. On the left is the goods yard access road. Note also Bedford "Wood End" Colliery in the background.

Photo, Alf Yates.

Plate 48. What would later become Class 25 under the TOPS re-numbering scheme, Type 2, No.5153, (no D prefix) crosses Holden Road with a short parcels train for Manchester on 3rd September 1968. *Photo, Ian Isherwood.*

Plate 49. A two car Metro-Cammell DMU in green and blue liveries, arrive at Leigh from Manchester Exchange on 14th May 1968. Note the cross-over in the foreground, used to reverse the Exchange-Leigh local trains.   *Photo, Alf Yates.*

Plate 50. An unusual viewpoint showing the elevated nature of Leigh Station as D5055 prepares to depart for Blackpool. On the right is the "Railway Hotel" on Bond Street, still standing but disused. Note also the BICC tower betwixt it, and the chimney stack. *Photo, Ian Isherwood.*

Plate 51. Another view in Leigh station on 25th May 1968 of Type 2, No.D5055, with the BICC, Blackpool excursion. These locomotives later became Class 24 under the Tops scheme and this example, No.24 055, re-numbered in February 1974. A number of BICC specials ran in consecutive years and on the evening of 3rd May 1969, when the last of the specials had returned, Leigh Station was closed and the town isolated from the rail network. *Photo, Alf Yates.*

Plate 52. On the last day of service, 3rd May 1969, a Trans-Pennine unit calls at Leigh with the 09.43 to Lime Street. This train had left Manchester Exchange at 09.10 and called at Eccles, 09.18, Monton Green, 09.22, Worsley, 09.25, Tyldesley, 09.34, and Leigh, arriving at 09.41, a time of 31 minutes. After thirty years of "progress" which saw closure of this and many other local railways, it is impossible to complete the same journey by road in anything approaching that timing during the normal working day.

Upon departing Leigh the train also called at Newton-le-Willows, Earlestown, St Helens Junction and Rainhill, then ran non-stop to Lime Street arriving at 10.25. *Photo, Alf Yates.*

Plate 53. A westward view at Pennington (W.Junction) in 1964, with a van parked near the site of W. Junction cabin. At this period through workings between Bickershaw and Pennington Junctions had ceased and the remaining single track used for cripple storage.

Photo, Tom Edmondson.

Plates 54 & 55. On 2nd June 1976, Class 47 No.47 344, leans into the curve at Abram en route to Bickershaw Colliery and, **in** *Plate 55*, having run round, is seen at the head of what is thought to be a test train for future MGR workings direct from Bickershaw. At this period all coal was despatched to the Exchange Sidings at Abram North by colliery engines, for collection by B.R. As can be seen, the wagons are empty and this single locomotive would not be able, unassisted, to get this number of loaded hoppers out of the "Hole".

The corporate blue livery is, with the advent of privatisation, becoming extinct, few locomotives are now to be seen in this colour. *Photos, G.Bent.*

Plates, 56, 57, 58. Some 10 years later a new rapid despatch bunker came into operation, as described in **"A Lancashire Triangle" Part Two,** and the gradient eased considerably. Bickershaw Colliery closed on 27th March 1992, and on that day Class 20's Nos.20 168/059 are pictured at the head of a MGR train loading for Fiddlers Ferry as Class 60, No.60 061 assists and, opposite, later seen near the former Park Lane level crossing on departure for Springs Branch. *Photos, Author.*

41

Plate 59. The scene at Abram North c1970, as D332 prepares to depart for Springs Branch with a load of Bickershaw coal. This locomotive became 40 132 under the TOPS re-numbering scheme having been built at Vulcan works, Newton-le Willows, entering traffic in 1961. Although withdrawn in 1982 the locomotive was not cut up until 1987.

Photo, Tony Oldfield.

Plate 60. In two tone green livery, Type 4 No.1824, later renumbered to 47 343, waits to depart Abram North Sidings with a coal train on 12th May 1973.   *Photo, G.Bent.*

Plate 61. To cater for the Merry-go-Round coal despatches which were to be operated by B.R. direct from Bickershaw, the entire branch, from the former Manchester Lines Junction at Spring Branch, to the new rapid despatch bunker at the colliery, was re-laid with welded rail in early 1985. On 9th March 1985, Class 20, No.20 176, is seen heading to Abram North with ballast hoppers. The photograph is taken from the Bickershaw Lane overbridge.

Photo, Author.

Plate 62. A site adjacent to Chequerbent Yard was taken over by J.K.Holt, scrap merchant, and a number of ex-colliery locomotives were cut up there. This view at Holts on 27th February 1986, is of *Harry*, Ex-W.D. No.71499, HC/1776/44, which had arrived at Holts in 1976 from Walkden Yard. There it remained, surrounded by a mountain of scrap, until 1992 when *Harry* was sold to the Shropshire Railway Preservation Society. *Photo, Author.*

Plate 63. At Gibfield Colliery Sidings, a location steeped within the history of the Bolton & Leigh Railway, former Wigan Coal & Iron Company locomotive *Crawford,* built in 1883, is seen in 1963, and is shot from the footplate of a passing locomotive working to Patricroft. *Crawford* had originaly been built with a short saddle tank but later received the tank from another of the company's engines, *Emperor* when the latter was scrapped in 1947. *Crawford* was scrapped at Gibfield in 1964. *Photo, J.R.Carter.*

Plate 64. February 1979 as *Warrior*, HE/3823/54, gives a spectacular display in the snow en-route from Bickershaw Colliery to Abram North Exchange Sidings.

Photo, D. Huntriss Colour Rail.

Plate 65. *Warrior* and her crew pause for conversation at the Bolton House Road level crossing on 29th August 1977. The livery of the locomotive shows up well in this view.

Photo, G.Bent.

Plate 66. With Bickershaw Colliery in the background, *Hurricane,* HE/3830/55, departs for Abram North on 2nd June 1976, also giving an atmospheric display.

Photo, G.Bent.

Plate 67. On 30th September 1971, Austerity *Spitfire,* HE/3831/55, is seen near the screens at Bickershaw between duties. *Spitfire* and *Hurricane* had both arrived new at Parsonage Colliery in September 1955 but both engines spent a great deal of their working lives at Bickershaw.

Photo, B.Magilton.

Plate 68. Austeritys *Spitfire* and *Rodney*, HE/3695/50, get to grips with the gradient between Bickershaw and Abram in the winter sunshine on 21st January 1970.

Photo, B.Magilton.

Plate 69. Opencast operations began at Bickershaw in 1975, on the site formerly occupied by Diggles Higher Hall Colliery. Sidings, a locomotive and a batching plant were provided by the N.C.B. Opencast Executive at the Albert Colliery site to receive the output from these workings. On 22nd December 1982, the Opencast Executive's 0-4-0 Senitel shunter is seen drawing forward toward Abram North Exchange Sidings with opencast coal for collection by B.R.locomotive. The opencast sidings ceased to be used for rail despatches after the disasterous mining strike of 1984/5 when, as in many other locations, coal traffic had gone over to road transport. *Photo, Author.*

Plate 70. The Barton Wright Class 23 locomotives first appeard as 0-6-0 tender engines in 1877 and were subsiquently re-built by Aspinall as 0-6-0 saddle tanks from 1891 onward. This example, L.M.S No.11456, had been sold to Coppull Colliery c1937/8, arriving at Parsonage from Ince Moss Colliery in 1961. On 24th April 1968, the locomotive is seen being towed by one of the Yorkshire Engine Company built diesel shunters across Westleigh Lane, Leigh, en-route to Howe Bridge West Sidings for onward transportation by B.R. to Ellenbrook Sidings and eventual preservation. **See also Plates 169, 400 & 401, A Lancashire Triangle.**   *Photo, the late B.Hilton.*

Plate 71. Austerity *Stanley*, HE/3302/45, takes water at Astley Green on 23rd March 1970, as stable mate *Harry*, HC/1776/44, engages in a spot of shunting. Production ceased at Astley Green from 3rd April 1970, but existing stocks continued to be moved until October. *Harry* was later sold to the Shropshire Railway Preservation Society, *Stanley* was transferred to Ladysmith Colliery, Cumberland c1970/1, being scrapped there in 1975.   *Photo, B.Magilton.*

Plate 72. A pair of Austeritys approach the camera in 1970, and are seen en-route from Astley Green to Astley Green Sidings with a heavy load.

Photo, Tony Oldfield.

Plate 73. Seen at Astley Green Colliery in the mid 1960's is 0-6-0 *Bridgewater,* HE/1474/24, which had been built for Manchester Collieries and saw service at a number of locations in the area, but spending the last ten years at Astley. It was cut up at Walkden Yard in October 1968.

Photo, J.R.Carter.

Plates, 74 & 75. A three-quarters forward view of *Respite*, HE/3696/50, which shows up the makers plate well, and the going away shot at Astley Green in the late 1960's. *Respite*, was noted laid aside at Walkden Yard in 1971. After being outshopped at Walkden the locomotive was transferred to Ladysmith Colliery, Cumberland, in November 1972, and later arrived at Bickershaw, via Walkden Yard in 1975 where it remained until 1981 when it was sold to Resco Ltd, Erith, finally arriving at the National Railway Museum, York, in February 1985.

Photo, D.Hill.

Plate 76. Here's our old friend *Harry* again seen approaching Mosley Common Colliery after the steep climb from Booths Hall Bank with coal from Astley Green about 1966, having recently been outshopped at Walkden. The East Lancs, A580, road is upper left.

Photo, J.R.Carter.

Plate 77. *Warrior*, HE/3823/54, passing Mosley Common Colliery en-route to Ashton's Field in January 1970, with coal for the blending plant. *Warrior* was, in all probability, the last steam locomotive to work this turn of duty.

Photo, B.Magilton.

Plate 78. Ellesmere Shed, Walkden, on 2nd January 1969. To the right a line of condemmed locomotives await the cutters torch. The colliery railway continues out of shot, far right, toward Hill Top and Ashton's Field.

Photo, D.Hill.

Plates 79 & 80. Opposite, *Harry*, HC/1776/44, approaches Walkden with a train from Astley Green bound for Ashton's Field in November 1968, assisted by *Repulse*, HE/3698/50. Mosley Common Colliery, which had closed in February 1968, is visible in the background.

Steam for effect ! as *Repulse* passes the camera.

Photos, D.Hill.

Plate 81. Inside Ellesmere Shed where *Warrior* has arrived at the end of shift whilst *Fred*, RSH/7289/45, hides in the depths. *Fred* departed Walkden for the Keighley & Worth Valley Railway in April 1969. *Warrior* was transferred to Bickershaw Colliery in mid 1977 and was eventually re-named *Fred* before being sold to the Dean Forest Railway in 1984. *Photo, B.Magilton.*

Plate 82. On a wet and murky 26th March 1966, a brake van tour of the Central Railway system took place utilising one of the ex-North Staffordshire 0-6-2 tank engines, *Sir Robert*. The ensemble is seen crossing Cleggs Lane, Little Hulton, as some of the participants admire the delecate scenery of the surrounding area !   *Photo, the late B.Hilton.*

Plate 83. Ex-North Staffordshire No.2, formerly *Princess*, is seen at Sanderson's Sidings in the mid 1960's and sports the "preserved" livery as applied by Crewe Works in 1960, prior to the locomotives exhibition at Stoke-on-Trent. Note the crest affixed to the upper cabside.

Photo, JR Carter.

Plate 84. The End., Bickershaw Colliery c.1992.

Photo, Author.

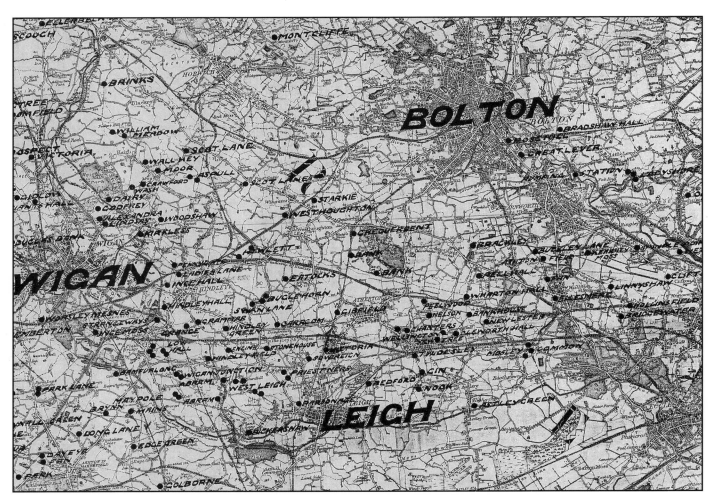

Railways and collieries in South Lancashire, early 20th century.